HERE & NOW
The Sacred Secular

The CHRISTIAN IDENTITY SERIES allows the modern layman to find meaning in the teachings of Christ, to help him anchor his personality in ageless values, to show him how christianity can be lived today. The series provides the layman with information about the human condition, the questions life raises, and the solutions that the gospel message can offer to existence. Since christian identity cannot be found in isolation, the series addresses itself to the total human community. It is designed for private reading, for classes in religious education, and for study groups. Each volume contains discussion questions, suggestions for further readings, and multi-media.

MATTHEW EUSSEN, EDITOR
Center for Studies in Religious Education

Here & Now

THE SACRED SECULAR

BY

James C. Chereso

CHRISTIAN IDENTITY SERIES

GEO. A. PFLAUM, PUBLISHER

DAYTON, OHIO, 1969

REVISORES ORDINIS
Cletus Wessels, S.T.D.
Matthew Eussen

IMPRIMI POTEST
Clement E. Collins, O.P., Provincial

NIHIL OBSTAT
Cletus Wessels, S.T.D., Censor Deputatus

IMPRIMATUR
✠ James J. Byrne, S.T.D.
Archbishop of Dubuque
August 20, 1969

PHOTO CREDITS
Alan Oddie: Page 72; Paul Tucker: pages 14, 19, 24, 30, 38, 42, 49, 58, 64, 78, 86, 96, 104, 122; Edward Wallowitch: page 8.

Library of Congress Catalogue Card Number: 79-97045

GEO. A. PFLAUM, PUBLISHER
38 West Fifth Street, Dayton, Ohio 45402

Manufactured in the United States of America

Contents

1: A SECULAR THEOLOGY   9

2: A SECULAR OUTLOOK   25

3: A SECULAR GOD   43

4: A SECULAR CHRIST   65

5: A SECULAR CHURCH   87

6: A SECULAR LITURGY   105

     SUGGESTED READINGS   123

     MULTI-MEDIA   125

HERE & NOW
The Sacred Secular

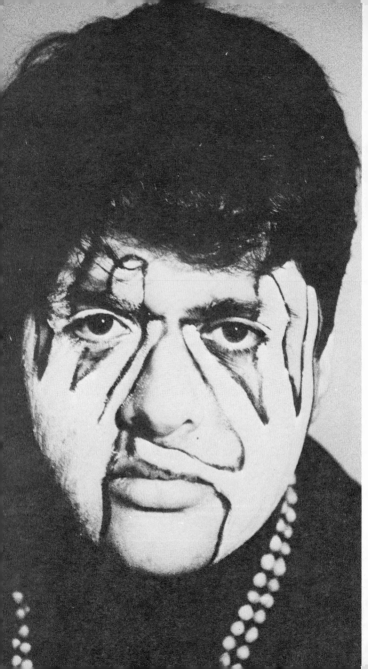

1

A Secular Theology

The most commonplace remark today is that the most conspicuous phenomenon of our time is change. And while gradual and sometimes imperceptible change (evolution) has always been the basic ingredient of nature's way and the way of man and his society, history has also recorded the staccato eruptions of that species of change called revolution—both of the violent and nonviolent variety. There has been no sphere of human living which has been immune to revolution. Time and again it has affected politics, economics, science, art, philosophy, and religious institutions.

Secular theology claims to be a reflection of, and a comment on, the revolution taking place in our time. A process of secularization is so transforming man and his institutions that, in order for the christian gospel to be the leaven, it ought to be in the modern world

and it must be given a new reading. The old
reading emphasized the future life in another world. The new reading turns the old
one on its head. The emphasis is on *now* and
this world. This new reading of the gospel
is producing new modes of christian thought,
action and worship, as I will try to show.

We can begin to describe the process of
secularization by another commonplace observation of today: we are experiencing a
generation gap, one that seems completely
different from other such gaps in the past.
There was a time—as ancient as that of
Plato and as recent as that of Einstein and
the 30's, even as recent as that of the 40's
and 50's—when adolescents and young adults
looked upon their parents, uncles, aunts and
teachers as old-fashioned. But those times
also saw the same adolescents and young
adults grow up and gradually admit that
their parents were "right after all," and that,
"well, you know, you've got to settle down
and think about *your* children and responsi-
bilities."

The beginning of this change occurred
when the twelfth century acclaimed the *ars*

mechanica, that is, technology. Later, technology began keeping pace with the great strides of science introduced by Copernicus, Galileo, Newton and Darwin. Now it is upon us, full-blown, in this age of electronics. Adolescents and young adults are speaking a language and thinking thoughts and verbalizing a future in forms that baffle, worry and irritate their elders. These young people are simply *not* about to capitulate to, nor join the "old" culture of the immediately previous generation.

Just what kind of a force in society do young people of this decade make up? The temptation is a nagging one: aren't these young people just another version of young people in any decade of the past? In attempting to answer this question we can go back to the youth of the 1950's. That college generation was alienated, but it was culturally passive. It never presented a serious challenge to the adult culture. The student put in his four years or more of college with the serious intent of getting ready to fill his own place in an already-existing culture. Today, on the other hand, while the youth are also alienated from adult society, they are culturally active. They are becoming more and more responsible for cultural innovations in America and elsewhere in the world. We cannot avoid noticing that much of what is new and exciting in art, entertainment, fashions, education, politics and morals find its inspiration in our discontented youth and in those who identify with them. Our best minds— for good or ill—are more and more taking their cues from this sub-culture.

An analogy suggests itself here. The early christians in second-century Rome were generally thought of as poor, irreligious, seditious, revolutionary, draft-dodging, and a threat to law and order. But, they spoke of humility and gentleness and love! The analogy, however, does not extend only to the externals. These early christians penetrated and subverted the very foundations of Roman society, and it seems our youth are doing the same in our society.

We may ask, what kind of a force do these young people represent? About half of our population is made up of those twenty-five years old and under. Within a few years, one

out of every three Americans will be in
school. Moving beyond our own country,
within thirty years, sixty per cent of the
earth's population will be comprised of those
under twenty-one. A great majority of the
youth in that time will absorb, with efficiency
and a minimum of effort, an intellectual heri-
tage which is available today to only a hand-
ful of intellectuals.

The minds of today's youth are already
affected by space travel, atomic power and
weaponry, automation, wonder drugs, meth-
ods of expanding consciousness, molecular
biology, laser beams and supersonic jet trans-
port. Older people, those brought up in a
milieu of nationalism, rationalism, other-
worldly piety, and linear and literal thinking,
must catch up, adapt or perish.

Today's youth seem to have, in regard to
the present and the future, the clear vision
and risk-taking desires that have always been
a part of the christian gospel. Even if today's
youth cannot lead us to a new christian culture because they are still dependent on
their elders in so many ways, at the very
least they are playing a prophetic role. It is

the intent of this essay in secular theology to explore the implications of these prophecies with regard to some new approaches to God, Christ, church and liturgy.

It has been argued that secular theology has a fairly simple point to make: Jesus and the church are in and for the world. Having made this point, contemporary theology can move to other interests. I would argue against this view that secular theology is more than just a movement within the history of christian theology. It is also a method, that is, a way of "doing" theology, that is necessary for every cultural period. To say that theology must be secular is to say that theology must speak for, and to, the world in which it finds itself. The gospel must confront and be confronted by the world as it is today. This book will attempt to show that today's world is undergoing a process of secularization which demands a theology of secularization. We might even say that secularity is the mood which provides our period with categories of thought, valuation and action. In plain language, this is our immediate goal.

It is not uncommon for an unbelieving secular humanist and a christian secular humanist to work side by side in rendering self-sacrificing service for the upbuilding of the world and man. It is true that the two differ in their interpretation and understanding of the world and man. The christian envisions a goal for the world and man which is pure grace, while the goal sought by the nonbeliever is only this-worldly. But even the christian ideal fails to yield a practical difference between the work of the believer and nonbeliever.

As we shall see, the incarnation is not the deification of the world, but the very assurance of its worldliness. Looking for a uniqueness in Christ's message to the world often leads to the erroneous view that God intends the world to be different in the redemptive incarnation than it originally was in his creation of it.

The church's mission is not to christianize the world, but to allow it to emerge and become fully itself. The eschatological or graced future for the world is not the work of man, but of God making perfect and crowning the work of men, that of non-believers as well as that of believers. If the two do not differ with respect to the human goal, is there any *practical* difference?

We must understand the urgency of this fundamental question. The nonbeliever may say, "I see your picture of a God creating the world and then renovating it in his Son and pulling the whole thing toward himself in a future kingdom of light and love and peace. But all this sounds like a myth to me. What is important is to get back to the job of making something of this world." The point of the nonbeliever is simply this: not only scientific statements but especially theological ones are meaningless unless we can find some verification for them in empirical experience. What might this concrete experience be? Where shall we begin to look for it?

I suggest, at least as a beginning, that the concrete experience is one of hope for the future of the world and man. Let us see first what is available to the nonbeliever as a basis for hope. Later we shall see what is available to the believer.

The long history of mankind makes it pain-
fully clear that the progress of a completely
autonomous humanity, that is, one lacking
the faith-vision of a transcendent goal and
purpose, is continually being vitiated and
even sometimes negated by moral regression,
the domination of evil over good, and the
prospect of facing a death bearing the promise of nothing to human eyes that will be
finally closed to the light of life. These real
evils are a constant source of temptation to
the nonbelieving humanitarian. His ardor for
service is very apt to cool. He may even
withdraw to an individual existence, despair-
ing of finding any meaning to reality at all.

The christian's hope is not blind to the
world's regression and evil or to the inevi-
tability of death. But his hope rests on Jesus
who *is* the world's progress toward the future, on Jesus who has already conquered
evil, who, by dying, won for himself and for
all men the risen life. While christian faith
says that the world and man have an absolute future which is humanly impossible to
achieve, christian hope says that the humanly
impossible becomes possible in Jesus. Even

the limited goals of humanitarian work usually end in failure, as history shows and the doctrine of the Fall explains, without the dynamism of christian hope.

When we have isolated the hope of the christian as contrasted with the nonbeliever's lack of hope, do we have any empirical evidence which can verify our christian interpretation of reality? There is none except the immediate experience in the very person of Jesus who is the foundation of christian hope. This hope is even more immediately founded on the love for the world which God has manifested in Jesus: "God loved the world so much that he gave his only Son" (Jn. 3:16). God's love for the world continues to be made manifest in the christians' love for one another in the church and especially in the church celebrating the eucharist.

While this love of God in Jesus is manifested by the church in her day-to-day service to the world, it is especially manifest, and hence available to the experience of the nonbeliever, during the eucharist, providing the Spirit chooses to inspire his mind and heart at this time. This love of God in Jesus in the church is especially manifest then because it is then specially celebrated. It is on such an occasion that our unbelieving secular humanist might identify himself with the Baptist's two disciples who were following Jesus one day out of curiosity. "Jesus turned round, saw them following and said, 'What do you want?' They answered, 'Rabbi, where do you live?' 'Come and see,' he replied; so they went and saw where he lived, and stayed with him the rest of the day" (Jn. 1: 37-39). It is often the simple situation that provides the special occasion.

If this occurs, then Christ will also remain with him as he did with his disciples who, after the death and burial of Jesus, had gone back to their fishing on the Sea of Tiberias as is related in Jn. 21:9-12: ". . . And there stood Jesus on the shore, though the disciples did not realize that it was Jesus. . . . The disciple Jesus loved said to Peter, 'It is the Lord. . . .' As soon as they came ashore they saw that there was some bread there, and a charcoal fire with fish cooking on it. . . . Jesus said to them, 'Come and have breakfast.' "

SOURCES

Bloy Jr., Myron. "Culture and Counter-Culture," *Commonweal*, LXXXIX (January 17, 1969), 494.

Byron, William. "The American Church in the Year 2000," *America*, 120 (January 11, 1969), 38.

Hurley, Niel. "The Church's View of the World," *America*, CXX (January 11, 1969), 47.

McBrien, Richard. "Secular Theology," *The American Ecclesiastical Review*, CLIX (December, 1968),399.

Schillebeeckx, Edward. *God the Future of Man.* New York: Sheed and Ward, 1968, pp. 193,197.

DISCUSSION QUESTIONS

1. What are some changes in present world society which are affecting the church?

2. Can revolution be nonviolent?

3. Does exclusive concentration on this world necessarily lead to a forgetfulness of religion?

4. Have you experienced in yourself or observed in others a change in attitude in regard to the church? Give some examples.

5. Have youth today decided that the values they want to work for are not the same as

those held by their parents and others of the older generation?

6. Is the mood of secularity really prevalent to-day? How would you describe this mood?

2

A Secular Outlook

In the past, when man's environment appeared as mysterious and even threatening, religion and philosophy explained that environment as being peopled by occult forces which could be either benign or malignant. Secularization is the process whereby man, in becoming more and more the controller and manipulator of his environment, is liberated from such religious and philosophical views. The evidence is from the study of primitive peoples and the progress of man. Extraordinary events which once required fate, chance, fortune and other phenomena for an explanation, have been scrutinized by natural science as events for which there is a natural explanation.

The secularization process can be seen with reference to institutional religion. Formerly, an individual did not join a church. He was born and raised in a society which was defined and unified by certain beliefs and rituals. Religion was collective and coterminous with the social body. Education of the young meant initiation into, and training in, the beliefs and rites of the whole community. Religion permeated all the customs and activities of group activity.

Then came the greatest change that has ever occurred in the history of religion: a shift in the social center of gravity of religion. This shift accompanied the enormous multiplication of non-ecclesiastical associations in the fields of education, politics, economics, science, culture and even philanthropy. Men in politics and economics and art were no longer clerics belonging to the structure of the church, but men who happened also to be members of a church. In short, there appeared an extension of interests which, from the viewpoint of religion, were nonreligious. The conditions under which people met and acted together were, as a result, profoundly modified.

The causes of this profound modification were, indirectly, theoretical science, and more directly, invention and technology as applied to industry and commerce. The social changes that have come about through these causes affect all people, whether they are aware of it or not, since instant communication has made of this world a global village. Even though religious fundamentalists have conceptions of man, of heaven and of earth which have remained unchanged since Copernicus, Newton and Darwin, even up to Einstein, yet their everyday life of politics and economics has been radically changed by the applications of science.

The resulting gap between religion and life may cause considerable uneasiness. The point of the foregoing is not so much that new organizations and activities have become independent of church control, but that new interests and values which, practically speaking, are unrelated to the church, are absorbing even the members of those churches.

Let us grant that the church-member may carry the ideals of his religion into his educational, recreational, political and economic activities. There are still two facts which indicate a secular revolution. First, this ac-

tivity is from personal choice and not moti-
vated by wish of the church. Second, an individual carries his personal beliefs into areas
that are essentially secular, that is, outside
and beyond the boundaries of religion. This
constitutes a radical change, although the
church's missionary aim still is to christianize
the market place. Even if ecclesiastics were
to try to claim that these new movements
find their origins in the church, one can agree
and at the same time see the new movements
go their own independent way.

This brief historical sketch of secularization presents us with the problem of defining
the relationship existing between the sacred
and the secular, the holy and the profane.
It will be useful for subsequent discussion
to begin with a distinction between "secularity" and "secularism" (the adjectives, "secular" and "secularist" correspond respectively
to the two nouns). Secularity can be taken
to mean, in particular, the world view of
modern science; and, more generally, as those
attitudes which are characterized by a concern for this world as opposed to the next.
These attitudes today prevail among all civi-

lized peoples, yet they are not necessarily inimical to belief in God. It is secularism which excludes this belief because it assumes that *only* science can give us real knowledge and *only* this world really matters at all.

Perhaps the best way of seeing the meaning of the secular and its relation to the sacred is to describe the extreme form of secularity which we call secularism. Secularism is not a philosophy. It is rather a pre-rational basis for such contemporary philosophical movements as naturalism, relativism, and evolutionism. Those movements tend consistently to an exclusive concern for the here and now, the sensible, the manipulable, the relative—in short, for the this-worldly. It is this tendency which unites them in a more general characteristic that can be described as a loss of the sense of ultimacy. Secularism, then, is a way of looking at reality and is found in many different areas of thought and of action.

But an even more detailed description of secularism can be made by locating those areas of life called secular. In such a description, the secularist is someone who thinks and

acts more or less exclusively in these areas. Moreover, the kind of religion the extreme secularist rejects are the extreme forms of religious expression which have earned the pejorative names of "religiosity" or "pietism." And if both extreme secularism and pietism look like caricatures, nevertheless they are part of the current scene.

We hope to see that a viable secular theology will not be one that accepts either extreme, but rather one that finds its center in a dialectical tension between the secular and the sacred. There are four areas in which the secularist and the pietist collide.

First, the secular is the temporal as opposed to the eternal. In fact, the Latin word, *saeculum,* from which our word derives, means "the present age," "the present generation"; it can also mean "history," that is, human activity in time. The secularist is concerned with the world here and now, with government, politics, social and economic problems. He is so concerned that nothing else matters—certainly not life in the next world. The secularist justifiably criticizes the pietist for being so concerned with his own salvation and the next life that he fails to shoulder his responsibility to work for the solution of the human problems of this world.

Second, and in a more general sense, the secularist is the very opposite of the pietist. The secularist is taken up with the daily activities of eating, sleeping, procreating, relating with one's neighbors, engaging in business, politics, art and recreation. The pietist, on the other hand, spends most of his free time praying, worshiping in common, fasting and meditating. The secularist criticizes the pietist for abdicating from real life and real concerns, maintaining that one can have an appreciation of goodness and beauty and a concern for social justice without removing oneself from the sphere of the secular or from the world.

Third, in the field of intellectual endeavor, secular knowledge is gained by direct observation, rational argument and practical testing. The secularist believes that religious knowledge or theology is removed from life and based on some kind of metaphysical principles which have no empirical verification. Such a position is usually a positivist one in that it asserts that only the natural sciences can give us reliable knowledge, and that even such disciplines as sociology and psychology, only yield true and useful knowledge to the extent that they approximate the method of scientific inquiry and measurement. Not only is theology dismissed as pseudo-knowledge, but it is also considered by some scientists as obstructive of the advance of true knowledge because of religious prejudices. An example of this would be religious disapproval of experimenting with test-tube babies.

Fourth, secularist man is autonomous. There is no higher being than man nor any deposit of revelation which gives man knowledge unattainable by human reason. By his reason man creates his own values, sets his own standards, determines his own goals and works out his salvation completely on his own. The religious man, on the other hand, is dependent on and obedient to a supreme being who may reward or punish him. The secularist sees this religious man as an immature human being, not yet completely fulfilled as a man.

Having contrasted these extremes, let us try to discover the true relationship between the sacred and the secular which might serve as the foundation for a secular theology which could also be authentically christian.

If we understand the sacred as religiosity and the secular as secularism, then there is a sharp dichotomy between the two. But religion and secularity can coexist in a creative tension. I hope to establish this in a more concrete way later on when I show that there is no real opposition between authentic christianity and secularity. In fact, I will show that the truly religious man is one in whom the tension between the sacred and the secular exists in a creative way. For the moment, let us explore the more general relationship between the sacred and the secular.

It is very important that the reader be not misled by the terminology. A dichotomy exists between the sacred and the secular only in the extreme life-styles of the pietist and the secularist. Otherwise, the sacred and the secular are not dichotomous, but are mutually inclusive.

The distinction between the sacred and the secular ought to be construed as vertical rather than horizontal. This means that we give attention to the depth of what concerns us rather than to *what* we are concerned about; what is significant, in other words, is *that* we are deeply concerned, whether it be about sports, social justice, sex, world government or the world-to-come.

This vertical view allows us to speak of two perspectives on everything: a religious (sacred) perspective which regards a thing completely and ultimately (that is, the thing as related to the supreme object of one's commitment), and a nonreligious (secular) perspective which regards the same thing partially and proximately. Engaging in a sport, for example, can be looked at as a means of keeping fit (partial and proximate goal) and as a means of keeping fit in order to practice a life of serving love (complete and ultimate goal).

This vertical view also suggests that we look at the sacred and the secular as dimensions rather than as compartments, since the latter are mutually exclusive while the

former are not. Thus, engaging in a sport
may be in a compartment of life but it has
at least two dimensions. In other words, *any*
person, thing or event can be seen in a finite
and proximate secular dimension, and in an
infinite and ultimate sacred dimension. This,
then, is what we seek when we begin looking
for depth in our concerns.

And yet the compartment distinction can
be useful. For there are certain objects and
acts which are specially set aside because
of their power to call forth a religious response and to provide a deep insight into
the meaning of life. The Bible, the sacra-
ments, the liturgy and other rituals have this
kind of power; playing golf does not. But it
can occasionally happen that some sacred
objects and acts lose their symbolic power
and that others once considered as secular
can become sacred.

There are four possible ways that the
sacred and the secular, while mutually exclusive if put in compartments, are also found
together as two different dimensions of the
same thing, as can be seen in the following
table.

1. Compartment of the *secular* secular (the secular in its secular dimension)	2. Compartment of the *sacred* secular (the secular in its sacred dimension)
Finding new sub-atomic particles	Intuition of the boundless possibilities of knowledge
Changing nonliving matter into living matter	Heightened sense of the mystery of life
Making a business decision	Profound experience of human freedom
3. Compartment of the *sacred* sacred (the sacred in its sacred dimension)	4. Compartment of the *secular* sacred (the sacred in its secular dimension)
Bible reading in church	Reading the Bible as human literature
Participating in celebration of mass	Attending mass in a routine, superstitious way
Visiting Christ in those who are in prison	Visiting a prisoner from a nonreligious motive

In regard to worship of God (not confined here to christian worship) we can say of the combinations in the above table that the first is not worship in any sense; the second does not involve religious symbols but it is worship in a basic sense because it is an experience opening out to the infinite and transcendent; the third involves accepted religious symbols which have the power to inspire explicit and formal worship; and the fourth is worship in outward appearance only because the symbols and rituals are lacking religious substance. Then, too, for most people, the greater amount of time is given to the first, with a little time set aside (once weekly?) for the third, and then this third has the value at the very least of reminding people that their preoccupations with the first imply an ultimate commitment. And while the second compared with the third lacks the explicit reference to the sacred— a reference found in specifically sacred symbols—it nevertheless has the advantage of making worship relevant to life, especially in an age when it is difficult to feel awe over holy places when we have men walking on

the moon. And as shall be shown later,
entrance into the holy places may be through
the sacred secular.

In conclusion, man is called upon not to
choose either the sacred *or* the secular, but to
maintain within himself and in his activities
that creative tension between the two which
will enable him to attain to the ultimate
source of both the sacred and the secular—
an ultimate we can experience and talk about
because it is a *secular* God.

SOURCES

Dewey, John. *A Common Faith*. New Haven and
  London: Yale University Press, 1934, pp. 60-66.
Macquarrie, John. *God and Secularity* (Vol. III of
  New Directions in Theology Today, Hordern, W.,
  ed.). Philadelphia: The Westminster Press, 1967,
  pp. 20-21, 43-49, 59.
Phenix, P. H. *Education and the Worship of God*.
  Philadelphia: The Westminster Press, 1966, pp.
  18-24.

DISCUSSION QUESTIONS

1. Are you a christian just because you were born of christian parents and were raised in the christian church?

2. Give some examples of the attitude of religiosity which you might have detected in yourself and observed in others.

3. Give some examples of how the church has obstructed intellectual progress.

4. Give some examples of beliefs and practices which are based on the idea that there is a dichotomy between the sacred and the secular.

5. Give other examples (see table) of persons, things, and events which have a sacred as well as a secular dimension.

3

A Secular God

The first half of the decade was startled to hear a repetition of the nietzschean pronouncement that God is dead. This declaration was not confined to theological and academic circles. It was communicated to the general public in such widely circulated news media as the *New York Times, Time Magazine, The New Yorker,* and in many other periodicals, radio, and TV. I shall point out here the more immediate reasons for the proclamation of the death of God, what it can possibly mean, and whether perhaps a living God who is also a secular God is much more credible than the God who lives in the popular, theistic belief.

The immediate occasion of the proclamation of God's death is the false dichotomy between the sacred and the secular. This false dichotomy resulted from a lingering religious fundamentalism, also in neo-

orthodoxy's insistence on an utterly transcendent God, liberalism's immanentist God
(God is equal to world process), and an
eccentric interpretation of Bonhoeffer's pro-
posal of a "religionless christianity." On one
side of the dichotomy, in reaction to the
"totally other" God of neo-orthodoxy, there
is radical secularism. In holding that science
can explain and do anything and that man
creates his own values and destiny, this
radical position so stressed the autonomy of
man that God was gradually faded out of the
universe. The result was a loss of the sense
of ultimacy. While it has been a perennial
problem of theology to speak of God as *both*
transcendent and immanent, the secularist
has opted for a total immanentism for this
present world, saying in effect: "You may call
the whole thing God if you want." On the
other side, religiosity, in reaction to immanentist liberalism, stressed that God and
all religious things exist separately from, and
over against, the world and all things secular.

In either case God is most certainly dead.
If he is identified with the world of man,
why even speak of God? But if he is *a* sepa-

rate being—even though supreme among other beings—who is "up there" or "out there" (and the Russian cosmonaut who didn't bump into God out there perfectly expresses the reaction to this belief), then it is difficult to say that he is truly living and in the world. If we supposed that God is only one being among many, one part of the whole of reality and therefore less than the whole of reality, he would not be worthy to be considered God or to be worshiped as such.

It is not necessary that we choose between these two extremes. We can still believe in a transcendent God against the radical secularist without accepting the transcendent God of popular theistic belief. Before offering some new language about God, rooted in true, theological tradition, let us first see the possible meanings of the phrase, "death of God," and the special meaning attached to the phrase by three modern "death-of-God" theologians. I will also offer a brief criticism and try to discover the reasons why the phrase has become a slogan.

There are four possible meanings of the phrase, "God is dead." First, it could mean that modern man has lost his inner-awareness of God, that man is coming to understand himself without recourse to the hypothesis that God exists. If this is the meaning then man's religious experience is dead, not God.

Second, it could mean that the political, economic and educational institutions which shape our consciousness are no longer based on the God-premise, and that christendom is dead. This is a sociological comment on our present society, saying in effect that we are in a post-christian era, which is not a comment on the existence or nonexistence of God. If God exists but is unknowable psychologically or sociologically, we are tempted to say with Sartre: whether God exists or not, he is of no use to us.

Third, it could mean that our current language and symbols do not know how to express the ultimate Reality who unifies all other reality and intervenes in history as a provident personal God. The world-view of christendom which formerly furnished us with language and symbols is gone. The present world-view—empiricist, scientific, technological and capitalist as it is—considers any language or symbol which tries to express extra-spatial and extra-temporal reality as meaningless. Here, too, this may be considered an ontological comment on our language and system of symbols rather than on God's nonexistence. If we cannot speak of God, how can we believe in him?

Fourth, it could mean that even the God of revelation—a self-revealing God given to us *beyond* our own ability to know—is a problem to us. In other words, psychological, sociological, and ontological difficulties with this idea of God have led to a revision of the notion of God. The God who was first known in a unique self-disclosure became a hidden God, an absent God, and finally a *dead* God. The result was to try to reformulate a theology which would no longer be based on God. This is an interesting venture, considering that "theology" literally means "the study of God."

Three recent theologians have chosen this path of renewing theology by basing it on other than God. T.J.J. Altizer insists that the death of God is an historical event, that God died by becoming totally incarnated in

Jesus Christ. He bases this on Philippians
2:5-11, but does not account for the statement, in the same passage, that finally all
men will confess Christ as Lord "to the glory
of the Father." This Pauline passage, in other
words, speaks of the *living* God who is glori-
fied when we confess his Son. But Altizer
insists that in speaking of the death of God
he speaks not of the God of idolatry, nor of
the God of false piety, nor of the God of
religion, but of the God of the historic christian church. However he recently stated that
"this talk about death was really the death
of neo-orthodoxy" (*Time*, May 2, 1969, p.
44).

William Hamilton is equally explicit. We
are faced in our generation, he states, with a
loss which is not simply a loss of idols or of
the God of theism. It is a loss of real transcendence. It is the loss of God. Hamilton's
claim to remaining a christian theologian is
that he still retains a "christological ethic."

Paul van Buren makes the same claim as
Hamilton. He does this after purging the New
Testament of all references to God. He is
able to make this purge because, on the

basis of an empiricist language-philosophy which he adopts, the question of whether God exists becomes a nonsense question. For just as the question, "Does X exist?" is a nonsense question when X does not stand for anything, so also the question about God, because the word "God" doesn't stand for anything at all.

One general criticism can be made of all three theologians. After proclaiming God's death, they all adhere to Jesus in an unconditional way. But one cannot be unconditionally committed to the historical man, Jesus, unless something unconditional appears in that man. To seek for this unconditional something is already to move in the direction of transcendence and God.

Why has the phrase "God is dead" become a slogan? First of all, because younger theologians felt an air of unreality in neo-orthodox talk about the "wholly other God"; "his stupendous saving acts"; "the encounter of faith"; and "the decisive eschatological event." Positivist accusations of meaningless language and existentialist affirmations of the absurdity of it all seemed to make much more sense. Secondly, it became a slogan because of the times. Attacks upon the *status quo*, the revolt of youth against their elders, student demonstrations and civil rights protests all had their influence. Whatever else it may mean, the death-of-God theology fits the present mood of activism and "getting with it," and represents a challenge to, and a break with, mainstream christianity in all its forms.

It is my thesis that mainstream christianity can accept this challenge because it can elaborate a doctrine of God which avoids the imagination of popular pietistic belief (that God is *a* supreme being "up there" or "out there") and which preserves the divine transcendence, discarded by the radical secularists. As I have already intimated, it is in the tension between the sacred and the secular, between the transcendent and the immanent, that there emerges a conception we can call "the secular God."

Thomas Aquinas never spoke of God as *a* particular being among other beings. He didn't even speak of him as a *supreme* being among other beings. He spoke of God as Existence Itself. Paul Tillich similarly speaks

of God as Being Itself, and the Ground of
Being. Not only is it impossible to imagine
or form a picture of Being Itself, it is also
impossible to conceive it by forming a mental
idea of it. This is because Being Itself is infinite and therefore defies being expressed by
a finite concept. This is why Tillich says that
to define God is to deny him. This is also
why Aquinas says that when we speak of
God we do not know what we are talking
about; that we do not prove the *existence*
of God but only that the proposition, "God
exists," is a true one; and that we can never
say what God *is* but only *what he is not*.

If our theological knowledge of God is so
negative—and even the Greek fathers considered theology as being "apophatic," that
is, "a denying theology"—then is it not better
to be agnostic and honest? The answer is,
"not necessarily," because there is a difference between *theological* knowledge of God,
and the knowledge which is a part of the
religious experience of God. We christians
believe that this experiential knowledge (and
the negating theology which it founds) is
available to us in Christ Jesus. While I will

speak more fully on this in the next chapter, I will pursue here, if only in general terms, this religious experience of the secular God based on the relationship I have traced between the sacred and the secular.

Note again the knowledge of God as it is conceived by popular theism. He is a supreme being, a person, who inhabits a supernatural realm apart from our world. He intervenes in events. He sent his Son from heaven. His Son went back to heaven and waits for us there until we are liberated by death. In the meantime we interrupt our daily life to raise our minds and hearts to God and his Christ "up there" or "out there."

Secular man cannot accept any of this. Such imagery of a *projected* God appears to him to be nonsense. Our generation looks at the universe non-dualistically. It sees the universe as one evolving reality. The God out there is simply not there at all. But while the secular man is thus not a theist in the popular sense, he is nevertheless a believer. He is trying to speak of God in a new way. What might this new way be? Where can it be found?

A new way of speaking of God will follow
a realistic recognition of just what kind of
experience of God is possible for us. We must
admit at the outset that, since God is absolute and infinite being itself, we cannot have
a direct experience of God. The only direct
experiences we have are of this world and
of man. In other words, if experience of God
is at all possible, it can only be *indirect*, that
is, through our experience of the world and
man. The question, then, is: Is there a real
reference in the world and man to God? If
there is, then an experience of worldly and
human reality will somehow also be an indirect experience of God.

The Bible clearly teaches that there is a
real reference to God in the world and man.
Not only is God the creator who looks upon
his creation as being "very good" (Gen. 1:
31), but he shows himself to be *for* the world
and man. This remains even after sin entered
into the world, when man became alienated
from himself, from other men, from the
world and from God. After sin, God entered
into a covenant with man and the world
because he still considered his creation to be

very good and therefore wanted to continue to act for it. In terms already agreed upon, it is God's act of *creation* and his active *concern* for the secular which imparts to it a sacred dimension.

While God intervenes in behalf of the world of man and leads his people from "the slavery of Egypt" to the freedom of his kingdom, he remains "hidden" and "absent." "Yahweh went before them by day in the form of a pillar of cloud to show them the way, and by night in the form of a pillar of fire to give them light; thus they could continue their march by day and by night. The pillar of cloud never failed to go before the people during the day, nor the pillar of fire during the night" (Ex. 13:20-22). It is important for our following discussion that we note that Yahweh went *before* the pilgrim people.

According to the Bible we have an indirect experience of God when we experience the sacred dimension of the secular present, a sacred dimension which gives the secular present its thrust toward the future kingdom. Moreover, this experience of God is ours

when we work unreservedly here and now
for the fulfillment of the secular present,
looking for the grace of guidance and power
from the God of the future (the "pillar" going
before us by day and night). This requires a
fuller explanation.

We experience God indirectly because the
experience of the sacred dimension of this
secular is based on the reference which the
secular bears to the God of our future. This
experience of the sacred dimension of the
secular comes to us when our empirical experience of some secular thing or event
discloses something that is deeper than the
experience of the secular itself. That experience discloses that deeper reality as the
ultimate condition and the basis for the very
possibility of the secular thing or event.

When we consider that God, who is the
ultimate condition and the basis for the very
possibility of the secular, is he who considers
the secular as very good, even after sin, then
the disclosure of the "sacred depth," which
is contained in our empirical experience of
the secular, becomes a reason for an existen-
tial trust in life. The disclosure is a basis for

the trust that, in spite of everything, in spite of man himself and the absurdity of it all, it is not evil but goodness that will have the last word after all. It is a trust that the future holds out the real possibility of being fully human and of the world coming fully to itself. It is a trust which leads to an experience of God-as-future, because we experience the *thrust* of secular things and events and people toward goodness and fulfillment in God and his kingdom. This thrust, the sacred dimension of the secular, is the result of the divine "pull" of the God of our future. He is the magnet.

Since human existence as a promise of "salvation" cannot be explained from *within* the secular dimension of that existence, we must place ourselves "on the boundary" between the secular and the sacred God of our future. The traditional proof of God from our experience of "dependency" thus becomes a rational justification for a conviction that already exists in us: that a meaningful worldly human future is neither an illusion nor a projection of wishful thinking. It is a conviction based on the experience in which

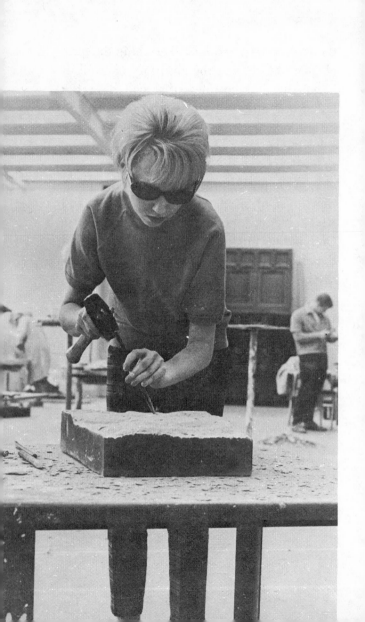

the God-who-is-to-come manifests himself as
absent, but nonetheless approaching.

His approach is felt when we experience
the depth of secular things or events—nature,
art, technological miracles, natural and man-
induced catastrophes. Secular things and
events can then be described as transparent
to the presence of a creative source holding
them together and conserving them in being
and beckoning them to future fulfillment.

This transparency of the secular to the
sacred is especially characteristic of inter-
personal relationships. Human existence as
"salvation" or the promise of being fully
human, summons us to work earnestly for
the betterment of the human condition in
this world at the present time. This means
that, despite bureaucracy and computers, one
has to work with human *persons*. It is here
that we experience, even though indirectly,
the living God. The "thou" or the persons
with whom we relate by loving is the window
through which we catch a glimpse of the
eternal Thou, because this Thou *is* Love. But
this Thou of Love is experienced only as the
ground and condition and very possibility

of our secular finite loves, since always he remains our Thou-of-the-future.

Man on the boundary between the sacred and the secular is neither overcome by radical secularism nor lured into a remote other-worldliness. We have said that the sacred and the secular are two dimensions belonging, not to two separate worlds, but to one world. The truly secular man, while living in the midst of material realities and human affairs, is at the same time living on the boundary. For this reason he can claim to see and treat these realities and affairs not only in their native dimension but also in the light of the Transcendent who is to come.

The feat of locating ourselves on the boundary is accomplished by our response of faith to the God who goes before us as our future. It is by reason of this faith, and it alone, that we can experience an indirect relationship with the eternal Thou. We cannot prove the objectivity of this experience, that it is not an illusion. We cannot even prove that the world is not absurd. We cannot, in short, eliminate the risk of belief in a secular God, faith in him.

Yet we face the challenge to take this risk. Jesus challenges us. It is here that we begin to understand a little better something of the absence and hiddenness of God who is the God of our future. God became man in order that we might know with certainty that, though he can be experienced only indirectly on the boundary between the sacred and the secular, nevertheless he himself has come to stand with us on that boundary. He comes to show us the boundary and stands there with us in Jesus who is his secular Christ.

Sources

Echlin, Edward. "God-Talk and the Now Generation," *The Homiletic and Pastoral Review*, LXIX (December, 1968), 183-188.

Gilkey, Langdon. "Secularism's Impact on Contemporary Theology," *Christianity and Crisis*, April 5, 1965, 64-67.

Hamilton, Kenneth. *God is Dead: The Anatomy of a Slogan*. Grand Rapids, Michigan: Wm. B. Eerdmans, 1966, 14 ff.

Hudson, Fred. "Four Meanings of 'the Death of God,'" *The Death of God Debate*, Ice and Carey, eds. Philadelphia: The Westminster Press, 1967, pp. 38-46.

Macquarrie, John. *God and Secularity* (Vol. III of *New Directions in Theology Today*, Hordern, W., ed.). Philadelphia: The Westminster Press, 1967, pp. 59-71.

Ogletree, Thomas. *The Death of God Controversy*. Nashville, New York: Abingdon Press, 1966, pp. 29-108.

Robinson, John. *Honest to God*. Philadelphia: Westminster Press, 1963, pp. 11-44, 53.

Schillebeeckx, Edward. *God the Future of Man*. New York: Sheed and Ward, 1968, pp. 71-75, 180-201.

DISCUSSION QUESTIONS

1. What are some of the characteristics of religious fundamentalism?

2. Have you ever had the feeling that God is dead? When and under what circumstances? What idea of God was presupposed to that feeling?

3. Is it possible to have a total commitment to Jesus if God is dead? Give reasons for your answer.

4. What is wrong with thinking of God as "up there" or "out there"?

5. How would you explain "a christianity without religion?"

6. Have you had any experience of the reality of God? Describe it.

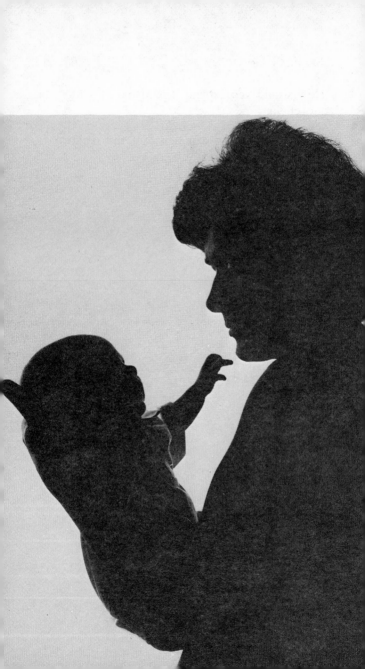

4

A Secular Christ

The Council of Chalcedon did not solve the mystery of Christ. When it spoke of Christ being constituted of a human nature and a divine nature and the person of the Word, the council only fully stated the mystery. This statement was uttered in order to forestall one-sided views of Christ: the view that he was *really* divine and only "appeared" to be human; or the view that he was *only* a man who realized in a special way what it means to be a son of God.

Although devotion to the humanness of Jesus was never absent in the church, there has always been present an overemphasis on his divinity and consequently a diminution of belief in the reality of his humanity. This one-sided view was nurtured by a dualism, a double principle which crept into christianity at a very early date. According to this doctrine the world and material things were

changing and unimportant and even evil,
while the world above was spiritual and eternal and good. This accounted for the wide-
spread ascetical practice of mortifying the
body, of subjecting the flesh to the spirit.
It also accounted for a general distrust of,
and withdrawal from, the world.

But there is a type of dualism which can
be authentically christian. It is the dualism
which takes into account the appearance of
sin after creation. What is the difference between these two dualisms? The false dualism is
ontological inasmuch as it posits two distinct
realities: one evil (this world) and the other
good (the next world). Christian dualism is
theological because it posits *one good reality*,
this world, but divided by sin—the state of
man's estrangement from self, from others,
from the world and from God.

This true dualism is reflected in such
biblical statements as: "The world was made
by him and the world knew him not" (Jn.
1:10); christians are to be *in* the world but
not *of* it (see Jn. 8:23, 15:18, 17:6); there
is a warfare between the spirit and the flesh
(see Gal. 5:17). But the church has often

overlooked this teaching of the Bible that there are two aspects to this world of flesh. It is both good and evil. It is good by itself but after the Fall it became infected with the evil of sin and all the consequences of that evil.

To the extent that the church has been influenced by the false dualism, it has viewed the process of secularization as just another repetition of man's continual apostasy from God and from his lawful representatives on this earth. It is also understandable how the church, under this same influence, has insulated itself from the mainstream of secular life and even opposed the progressive flow emanating from that life.

An example of this may be taken from the twelfth century. A suggestion was made at that time for making two rivers in Spain navigable in order to better the lot of the poor people in that region. A government commission answered the suggestion. If it were the will of God that these rivers should be navigable, he would have made them so himself; it would be a bold interference with the designs of Providence if human hands

were to try to improve what God, for in-
scrutable reasons of his own, has left undone.
Clearly, in a case such as this, and in many
other cases of more recent times, the church
does not say both "yes" and "no" to the world
of flesh as does the Bible, but just "no."

This simple no and black-and-white approach to the world of flesh is still common
within the church today. Unless we interpret
him wrongly, L. Brent Bozell, editor of the
conservative catholic monthly, *Triumph,*
seems to be a forthright spokesman for the
view that we are criticizing. "Christ put himself in stark, uncompromising opposition to
the ways of the world. He taught men to
turn to him, away from the world, or be
damned. He taught nothing else. . . . The
christian who urges the church to come to
terms with *this* world, with *this* age, is either
a victim of despair, or has ceased to be a
Christian at all" (*National Catholic Reporter,*
Mar. 22, 1967, p. 6).

The opposite extreme is more of a temptation for the post-Vatican II educated christian. Embarrassed by the church's uncompromising and uncritical hostility to the world,

this christian tends uncritically to celebrate
secularity without taking care to distinguish
between communicating with the world
(which is always good) and accommodating
to it (which is not always good). While the
conservative position is too simple and in-
secure, the liberal position is too uncritical.
The Bible itself maintains a certain tension
with, and ambivalence to, the secular, saying
yes to its goodness-potential and no to its sinful urgings.

The precise nature of this yes and no to
the secular will be considered in the chapter
on the secular church. But since the church
carries on the work of Christ, we must here
see *his* yes and no to the secular.

The biblical affirmation of the secular is
found in the doctrines of creation and incarnation. Christ plays a part in the former as
well as in the latter. Not only was Christ
present as the "spiritual rock" from which the
Israelites drank during their sojourn and
travels in the desert (see 1 Cor. 10:4), but
he was present at the foundation of the
world, because "the Word . . . was with God
in the beginning. Through him all things

came to be, not one thing had its being but through him" (Jn. 1:2-3). "And God loved the world so much that the gave his only Son" (Jn. 3:16). And the Word became a frail and mortal being and pitched his tent among us (see Jn. 1:14 and fns. m, n, in the *Jerusalem Bible*).

Chalcedon and the theology that followed that council paid much attention to what Christ was in himself—two natures in one person. But little has been done to clarify the relation of Christ to the whole of creation. While this relationship is quite explicit in the scripture just cited, it is more so in Ephesians 1:10 and 4:1-16, Philippians 2: 6-11, and Colossians 1:15-20. In these passages we find Christ's primacy over the universe and his central role in the creation and redemption of the whole cosmos. But if this pauline proclamation of the cosmic Christ and Teilhard de Chardin's christology in an evolving cosmos is today's great challenge in theological speculation, the idea of a thoroughly secular Christ, as opposed to the popular conception of a divine person who "dresses like a man," is also a challenge.

What is this yes and no of Christ to the secular? First, what is meant by the yes. Jesus is the truly human ideal for he is the man that God intends all men to be. By living in Christ through the Spirit, we are not taken out of the world but become more deeply involved in it, finding ourselves at the heart of it where we can truly love it and embrace it even in its darkness and pain. Jesus is the mediator between the sacred and the secular. This sacred is not necessarily opposed to the secular. It is a force that exists within the secular, compelling it to be itself. The sacred achieves itself only to the degree that the secular achieves itself, so that the emergence of an autonomous and creative secularity is the result of the yes of God, in Jesus, to his creation.

We must see all this as made explicit in the incarnation. In Jesus Christ, man and his world have been assumed in an "hypostatic" union. But God does not do violence to that which he took to himself. He does not do away with the "otherness" of the thing he assumed, but he took it to himself precisely as something other than himself. For God

has the power to call things into existence in such a way that their very dependence on him is transmuted into independence and autonomy, precisely because they are called into existence by the one, unique divine existence. God alone can create things which can stand by themselves before his face. To the extent that radical dependence on him increases, so does independence of him increase. It is only because God can assume something and still preserve its non-divinity, its humanity and its worldliness that he was pleased to create the world and then to assume it in the Word. The incarnation, then, is a liberation of the humanness of Jesus, and in him a liberation of the world and man to find their own proper existence in order to become fully themselves.

The example of human friendship may be of help here. The more that someone is accepted as friend by another, the more does he become himself and the more powerfully are his possibilities stirred to realization. In like manner, the assumption of the world and of man into the Word enhances their possibilities and guarantees that the world and

man remains entirely worldly and human,
and God entirely divine.

It is different with the gods of the ancient
Greeks who were rational principles of the
world, but within the world as deified parts
of it. Hence these gods were not entirely
divine, nor was the Greek world entirely
worldly.

To continue our example, the interpene-
tration of person and person in human love
is such that there is unity *in the very duality*,
without mutual absorption or reduction. How
this unity is achieved without mutual de-
struction of uniqueness, remains a mystery,
just as the assumption of the world and of
man into the Word also remains a mystery.
This way of thinking leaves no room for the
theology which would speak of the world
and man as deified in the incarnation, or of
the history of salvation as the gradual divin-
izing of the world.

What about Jesus' saying no to the secular?
God's descent into sinful flesh and his suffering on the cross is this no-saying. The
cross says no to the world and to man when
he seeks, in a flight of fanciful desire, to be

completely merged with the divine. The cross also says no to the world and to man when he would attempt to evolve the world into the kingdom of God by his own inner power, whether this be the kingdom of the enlightened mind, the fully civilized man, the classless society, or of whatever other kind. The cross says no to any secular power which would prevent the evolving of any secular reality *as secular*, because such power is the power of sin.

Returning to the discussion of Christ as secular, let me refer again to the example of friendship. The exemplar of the "love of friendship" between the sacred and the secular, between God and man and his world, where the secular is allowed to become completely itself, is the secular Christ. This is because Jesus was allowed, by reason of his very closeness to God in the Word and his "consubstantiality" with the Father, to become fully secular.

One thing is certain. Secular consciousness no longer feels comfortable with past theology which argued, quite independently of many passages in scripture, that "since Christ was true God, he couldn't have this thought or that desire or have done this or neglected that." Such a theology had the effect of changing the God-man into superman. Such theology also is not faithful to the "emptying christology" of St. Paul.

A fully secular Christ is not the result of the Word stripping itself of such divine attributes as omnipotence and omniscience. God does not perform the miracle of hiding his glory in Jesus. Rather, we have a fully secular Christ because Jesus emptied himself, not of his divinity, but of *himself,* so that he was able to become transparent to God (Jesus said, "He who sees me sees the Father," in Jn. 14:9). Thus is God able, in the secular Christ, to leave the world and assume the cross. He is able to appear weak and powerless in the world—the only way he can save man in the world (see. Mt. 8: 17). Pietistic man looks for the divine power of Jesus to help him, but the scriptures point to a powerless suffering servant, *the man for others.*

By assuming the human, the Word left that human in its complete autonomy. *How* the

Word was in Christ is a mystery. We can know only as much of the divine in Christ as we can know about God. If we recognize God on the boundary between the sacred and the secular, we are on that boundary *in Christ* who, as mediator between the sacred and the secular, *is* that boundary. If the center of man is God, the form or ideal of man is the form of the incarnate God and the incarnation of God is the unique supreme instance of the total self-fulfillment of the human being. It consists in this: that man *is* by giving himself away.

This is why our own humanity, in experiencing the risen life of Jesus, becomes, together with the scripture, the means of understanding the secular Christ. But we must read scripture (Mk. 5:30-33, for example) without theological presuppositions. We must also take the emptying theology of St. Paul seriously as God's way of having real solidarity with men as weak and sinful creatures. Only then will we not have to make excuses for the full humanity of Jesus, the limitation of his self-awareness, his need to make real human decisions about moral good

and evil, his real temptations, and the experience of his spontaneous human passions and affections.

If we find evidence in scripture that Jesus' knowledge was limited, the objection will be that, since there is only one person in Jesus, a divine person, the statement that Jesus had limited knowledge is the same as saying that the Word had limited knowledge. The answer to that objection can be borrowed from no less an orthodox or even ultraorthodox source than Cyril of Alexandria: "We have admired his goodness in that for love of us he has not refused to descend to such a low position as to bear all that belongs to our nature, *included in which is ignorance*" (*PG* 75, 369; italics mine).

After a very short public life of preaching the kingdom of God and doing good, during which time he was opposed and criticized as unclean, a left-wing radical, a threat to law and order, Jesus was condemned by the establishment of his time and put to death. These are the plain facts. Theological interpretation would embellish this by saying that Jesus knew that it was his last trip to Jeru-

salem and that he went *in order to* die, because the death of the incarnate God had
been decreed from all eternity as the means
of redeeming man. Such theology would be
consistent with the apocrypha which has the
boy Jesus playing with little wooden crosses,
and Mary looking on in deep dread and
with foreboding.

We can certainly follow the exegetes who
suggest that Jesus learned his mission and
identity the way he learned the language,
customs and religion of his people. He
learned gradually by confronting people,
things and events, by trial and error, and by
reflection on all his learning experiences.
Jesus came to realize that he was a mes-
senger of God whom he came to regard more
and more as Father. He had the important
work of reforming the religion of Israel and
of preparing men to spread to the whole
world the unique message that a life of self-
giving love and service to all men is necessary
and possible.

So Jesus journeyed to Jerusalem, not immediately to die for man's sins, but because
a prophet had to preach in Jerusalem, es-

pecially during the highly popular festival
days. He knew that he had enemies there and
could suspect a plot against his life, but he
went out of obedience to the message he had.
That obedience turned out to be "unto death
on the cross." The *way* Jesus accepted death
and the resurrection was for the disciples'
divine authentication of his life and message
and it led to their confessing that "Jesus is
Lord."

I have said that we come to know the
secular Christ from both scripture and the
experience of our own life in the risen Christ.
What does this mean practically? It means
that throughout history secular christians
must "show forth the death of Jesus until he
comes." This has happened again and again
in all those who have laid down their lives
in the selfless service of man, some more
spectacularly than others.

It has happened in our own time. On April
4, 1968, Martin Luther King, Jr., a man who
had already suffered much persecution in
fulfilling his christian mission to the poor and
oppressed, went to Memphis in spite of the
threat of death. He went to that place to give

support to striking garbage collectors. Martin
was then struck down by a bullet. He thereby
gave witness to the secular Christ in his
death as well as in his life. Jesus was crucified
again in Martin. Martin's death shows that
the merits of Christ's death are not separated
by geography and centuries of time and only
recalled by mystical ritual action. His death
shows that those merits are brought to bear
on our own times by secular christians such
as Martin Luther King who are obedient to
the call of self-sacrificing love—even to death
on a contemporary cross.

The difference between being religious and
being christian is the difference between being satisfied with only a ritual re-enactment
of Calvary and acceptance of the real cross
of living a life of secular service to men in the
world among Christ's poor and oppressed.
Here is the atonement and the resurrection
in secular form that borders on, and opens to,
the sacred dimension. Jesus must be seen as
fully and unashamedly human before his
lordship and divinity can be seen for the
unspeakable mystery that it is. God was
completely in the secular Christ "for in him

the complete being of God, by God's own choice, came to dwell" (Col. 1:19); and in Christ the complete being of the Godhead dwells bodily (cf. fn. to Col. 2:9 in *The New English Bible*).

If we have come to regard Jesus as the secular Christ, we must also look upon the church in a secular fashion, for the church is Christ's own body which continues his mission in the secular world of space and time.

Sources

Brown, Raymond. "How Much Did Jesus Know?" *The Catholic Biblical Quarterly*, XXIX (July, 1967), 37-39.

Clarke, Thomas. "The Humanity of Jesus," *Commonweal*, LXXXVII (November 24, 1967, special issue on Jesus), 237-241.

Dunne, John. "The Human God: Jesus," *Commonweal*, LXXXV (February 10, 1967, special issue on God), 508-511.

Lynch, William. "Toward a Theology of the Secular," *Theology Digest*, XV (Autumn, 1967), 176.

Megivern, James. "A Theology of Incarnationalism," *The Paradox of Christian Security*, Hargrove, K., ed. Englewood Cliffs, N.J.: Prentice-Hall, 1968, pp. 152-157.

Metz, Johannes. "The Christian and the World,"
Theology Digest, XIII (Summer, 1965), 96.

National Catholic Reporter, "Way to the Cross"
(Reporter Opinions Column), April 2, 1969, p. 3.

Rahner, Karl. *Theological Investigations,* Vol. IV.
Baltimore: Helicon Press, 1967, p. 111.

Robinson, John. *Honest to God.* Philadelphia: Westminster Press, 1963, pp. 74-75.

Schillebeeckx, Edward. *God the Future of Man.*
New York: Sheed and Ward, 1968, p. 55.

DISCUSSION QUESTIONS

1. What inferences would you draw from the
statement that Jesus was really a man and not
"God dressed up to look like a man?"

2. If Christ is the definitive revelation of God
and the center of reality, what about the
people who never heard of him because they
lived before he came?

3. Is our knowledge of the secular Christ only
from scripture?

4. What is the relationship of these three:
Christ's death, the mass, and christians?

5. Should Martin Luther King, Jr. be declared a christian saint (= hero)? Why or why not?

6. What do you understand by the faith-statement, Jesus is Lord?

5

A Secular Church

A secular church is not, first of all, one whose members are called upon to christianize the world, to change it into something other than it was, to overcome its native worldliness, to transform it into a sacred entity. Nor is a secular church one which imposes upon the secular certain a priori forms which are considered to be religious, an imposition hindering the secular world from taking its own shape and becoming fully itself.

A secular church is one whose members carry on the creative and redemptive work of God in Jesus Christ, the work of *secularizing* the world. We have seen that it is in the very act of creation that the secular is guaranteed its creative autonomy. This guarantee is reaffirmed and brought to definitive perfection, at least in promise, by the incarnation.

I say "at least in promise" because a secular church realizes its limitations. Sin has alienated the world from itself and has reduced it to a state of slavery. "From the beginning until now the entire creation . . . has been groaning," says St. Paul (Rom. 8:22). Since the world is totally comprehended by christianity, grace becomes the healer and perfector of the world. While the secular church is the visible, palpable sign of that universal grace, it itself does not comprehend the world, but strains, in hope, toward that comprehension which will be the eschatological kingdom.

A secular church imitates the descent of God into the world and carries on Christ's liberating assumption of the world. The body of Christ is what Harvey Cox calls God's *avant garde* in the world, discerning the action of God in the world and joining in his work. Matthew 25:35 tells us where that action is: in the hungry, sick, naked, thirsty and imprisoned people of this world. The people of God takes its very shape and assumes its own peculiar style precisely where God is acting. It joins in that action by performing three functions of service: preaching, healing and reconciling and being a sign.

A secular church advertizes that Christ has seized worldly power; he has already defeated the "principalities and powers," that is, the obstacles to the secular becoming fully itself, which are the enemies of human freedom and responsibility. By means of the cross, the church says no to the demonic secular and breaks down divisions, heals and reconciles wherever there are conflicts between the haves and have-nots, between ethnic groups, political parties and nations.

The church also functions as God's provisional sign of his intent for the whole of humanity, namely, that it be one in the kingdom of love and peace. In order to be this sign of unity for the whole human race, the church says yes to the goodness-potential of the secular by upholding the transcendent value of the human person and by promoting that brotherliness which is the sine qua non of dialogue. It is here that the secular church manifests both the incarnational and eschatological aspects of christian grace, inasmuch as it *even now* strives to achieve unity, personalism, and dialogue, all of which will at the same time *not yet* have reached their kingdom-fullness. (See Vatican II, *Pastoral Constitution on the Church in the Modern World,* nn. 33-39.)

A secular church takes its shape and assumes its style from where God is acting. God's activity is for *people,* not for the church as institution or organization. In brief, a secular church is world-directed. It has an all-consuming zeal and concern for the world of men.

It is in the light of this that we have to ask some disturbing questions. Does the church, as we know it, fit the above description? Does the present church still, in spite of Vatican II, concentrate on itself, its structures, its own preservation? Is its style in dealing with "subjects," often characterized by monologue, in issuing decrees from on high with no explanation of the reason for those commands and decisions? How did it become that way?

One may think that the church has for a long time been secular, inasmuch as it has organized itself after the sociological and political patterns of institutions in the world. But this meaning of secular is not to be applied to the church as the body of Christ. I shall show this by tracing the historical development of the structure of authority in the church.

Sociological analysis reveals that the present church is composed of superiors and inferiors. It is frequently the case that those who comprise the administrative elite discuss and decide issues among themselves, and then, in the name of authority, command subordinates to obey without question, reminding them that in so doing they are obeying the will of God himself. We may ask: Was this the authority structure of the first christian communities? Some of our ablest theologians, such as Yves Congar and John L. McKenzie, have argued that it is not.

The original *ecclesia* or church is described by St. Thomas as the "congregation of the faithful." And the faithful were those who, through baptism, became the people of God. Every person of that people shared in the priestly, prophetic and ruling functions of Jesus the founder. The community came before the hierarchy. The hierarchy grew from within the community, because bishops were elected by the whole community. The whole community contributed advice and insights for the councils. All this was derived from a principle of authority which animated the whole community: the Holy Spirit. Because of this special source of authority, there were not superior/inferior relationships in the primitive church. The leaders were not called "father," but "elders," because they imitated the leadership of Jesus who is the "eldest among many brothers" (Rom. 8:29; see Col. 1:15). Jesus himself once said, "You must call no one on earth your father, since you have only one Father, and he is in heaven" (Mt. 23:9).

The Holy Spirit, who is the real authority, is the Spirit of freedom; and he inhabited every person in the community. Special gifts were given to individuals for group leadership, but these gifts of the Spirit were always given for the sake of serving the community, and never for the purpose of lording over it. Jesus had warned, in delegating his own authority: "You know that among the pagans the rulers lord it over them, and their great men make their authority felt. This is not to happen among you. No, anyone who wants to be great among you must be your servant . . . just as the Son of Man came not to be served, but to serve, and to give his life a ransom for many" (Mt. 20:25-28). The authority of Jesus, then, is fraternal authority. Such authority is unique to the society called the christian community or body of Christ or the people of God. No other society—familial, political, commercial or professional—has such an authority structure.

It was during the reign of Constantine that bishops and priests were given special privileges and vested with public authority within the structure of the empire. It was a mutual thing. Constantine saw the usefulness of christianity for the unity of his empire. The church, represented by the hierarchy, saw the advantages of self-advancement and effectiveness in society by assuming the political structure of Roman law.* Whatever one may think about this romanization of the church, it was not in the least questioned at the time, for the chaos threatened by the barbarian invasions was averted by the church's appeal to the Roman conception of law and order.

The Roman spirit served the church and the social milieu well, but in a form other than that intended by Jesus. The church thereby became more secular in the sense of accommodating to the world, more juridical and more based on the ruler/subject relationship. Authority in the church now became something apart and sacrosanct, demanding to be served rather than fulfilling Jesus' command that *it* serve the faithful and the world. Moreover, additional honors, dignities and privileges granted to the clergy by the christian emperors following Constantine, in addition to the practice of celibacy and special dress adopted in the fifth century, made the gap between hierarchy and people even wider, so that at this time the clergy became a ruling class distinct from the rest of the faithful.

Then came the full-blown legalism of the late middle ages when the church was almost completely thought of in the restricted terms of the Roman pope and curia. This Roman authority, shared with other bishops and also with pastors and superiors of religious orders, was outside and above the simple laity (including in this latter group priests and religious "in the ranks"). Almost all those in authority, following the example of the Roman authorities, functioned as rulers, officials, patriarchs and directors, rather than as servants. From the eleventh century on, church authorities adopted the language, ceremonial and ideology of the imperial courts. Even today the close advisors of the monarchical papacy, the cardinals, are still called princes of the church.

The protestant reformation led the fathers of Trent to reaffirm and strengthen the then threatened authority-structure. They decreed that all subjects were to obey institutionalized authority unquestioningly because such authority manifests the will of God himself. Today, the teachings of Vatican II would have us return full circle to the fraternal authority-structure of the New Testament ecclesial communities.

This cannot be simply a return to the simple structure of the primitive church, because the church has since grown in size and scope. While I cannot attempt here to write a constitution for a renewed church, I can

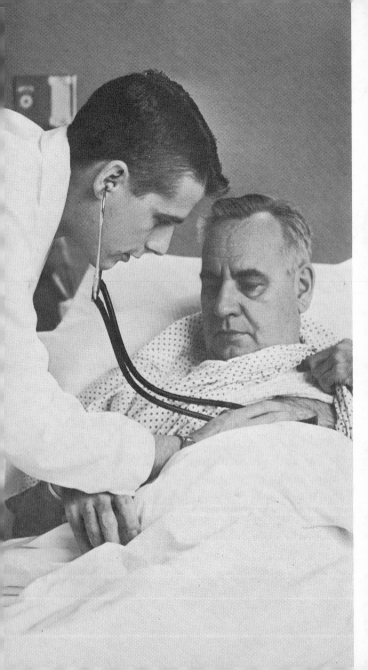

perhaps indicate in general terms some of its outlines. One aspect of the primitive church must be reinstated. The offices of pope, bishop, pastor and religious superior must no longer confer special social position, power, or wealth, but must become the happy onus of serving all the faithful and the world of man.

Vatican II spoke of collegiality as the form of authority which should exist in the church (see *Dogmatic Constitution on the Church*, nn. 22, 23). The implication is that *only* such authority is acceptable because it alone is evangelical, that is, characterized by the brotherly love of Jesus our brother who is the head of the church *as brother*. I have indicated the uniqueness of such authority in the world. Even a democracy's authority structure, close as it may come to resembling collegiality, cannot, in the end, be fraternal.

According to the principle of collegiality, leadership in the church derives its authority from the Holy Spirit who inhabits the whole church and each of the faithful. First, the principle means that the pope should exercise authority *in union with* the bishops who represent the local churches throughout the world. If this principle were thus implemented, the role of the pope would not be as absolute monarch nor would there be need of a college of cardinals and other advisors and officials in the Roman curia. Despite this, the council asserts that collegiality does not lessen "the Roman pontiff's . . . primacy over all, pastors as well as the general faithful. For in virtue of his office . . . the Roman pontiff has full, supreme and universal power over the church. And he can always exercise this power freely" (*Dogmatic Constitution on the Church*, n. 22).

Does this seem to be, in the same document, a watering-down of the collegial principle? It may be interpreted that way. The forging of the final documents of the council was often preceded by a give-and-take between progressives and conservatives. The references to the pope's undiluted primacy and his absolute power to make decisions without first consulting his fellow bishops may have been a concession made to certain traditionalist-conservatives among the fathers of the council.

I have noted that the principle of authority in the church is the Holy Spirit who inhabits all the faithful. This means that collegiality extends even beyond pope and bishops. For example, the bishops cannot know the entire local situation of their churches unless they are advised by their priests who are in immediate contact with the faithful. The priests in their turn cannot know the complete local situation and needs of the people unless they too consult with at least representative groups or individuals among the faithful themselves. In other words, collegiality would be shared in, in varying degrees, by *all* the members of the church, from the pope to and including the man in the parish. The final, practical decision-making in regards to the shape, style and apostolate of the local christian community would be made *on the scene*, and by those members immediately involved.

This decision-making could extend to the election of the hierarchy: for instance, the pope by a synod of bishops, the synod members by national councils of bishops, bishops by the priests and faithful of the local church, and priests by the people of an

individual community. In a sense, then, collegiality belongs to all.

All of the above is what is referred to and
included in the need for decentralization of
authority and the application of the principle
of subsidiarity. This would also require a
new and revised canon law for the *whole*
church consisting of *general norms,* allowing
the local churches to make more detailed and
flexible rules and regulations. These rules and
regulations would be prompted by local needs
and the concrete circumstances of the
apostolate, and not dictated in any a priori
way from on high.

I have said that a secular church is world-
directed and continues the work of God in
Christ, not by christianizing the world, but
by *secularizing* it, that is, by allowing the
world to become fully itself. This holds especially true for the *missionary* activity of
the secular church to non-christians. What
does this imply?

The secular church will no longer think in
terms of christian nations or a worldwide
christendom. The fact that these are dis-
appearing will lead to the secular church

being small, because future members will become so by a fully mature, personal decision, rather than by the mere accident of birth and milieu. Yet Vatican II has called the church "the sign of the salvation of the whole world." This means that, while the church is the visible, historical manifestation of grace, that grace is at work everywhere, omits no one, and offers God in Christ to all human beings. It also gives to the world an inner dynamic thrust toward the future kingdom of God.

The secular church, in its mission to non-christians, is not concerned with conversion as such, but rather with bringing them and their culture to their true development. It is the Holy Spirit, blowing where he will (see Jn. 3:8), who will be so present that grace, in its own due time, will work in them according to the tangible, concrete and historical forms it finds there, as it has already done in other communities in the church. In the meantime, the secular church will celebrate the present progress of true secularization of the world and rededicate herself to a continuation of that progress. The special occasion of that celebration and re-dedication is a secular liturgy.

SOURCES

"Christianity at the Heart of the World's Religions." *Herder Correspondence*, 3 (September-October, 1966), 274-281.

"The Christian of the Future." Herder Correspondence, 2 (July, 1965), 227-232.

Congar, Yves. *Power and Poverty in the Church*. Baltimore: Helicon Press, 1964, pp. 42-70.

Cox, Harvey. *The Secular City* (new revised ed.). New York: Macmillan, 1968, pp. 108-128.

DuBay, William. *The Human Church*. Garden City, N.Y.: Doubleday, 1966, pp. 158-159.

Kopp, Sister Mary Audrey. *The New Nuns: Collegial Christians*. Chicago: Argus Communications, 1968, pp. 33-45.

Megivern, James. "A Theology of Incarnationalism," *The Paradox of Christian Secularity*, Hargrove, K., ed. Englewood Cliffs, N.J.: Prentice-Hall, 1968, pp. 156-158.

McKenzie, John. *Authority in the Church*. New York: Sheed and Ward, 1966, pp. 27-61.

Discussion Questions

1. Is it wrong to criticize the church? What is meant by "church" in that question? Give reasons for your answers.

2. What changes would you like to see in the church? Why?

3. Is the present *form* of government in the church of divine origin?

4. What do you understand by "servant church"?

5. What do you understand by christendom? Should that be a goal of the church's missionary activity?

6. Why not just be a good christian—why belong to the church?

6

A Secular Liturgy

It is not God who needs worship, but *we* need to worship God. This assertion of St. Thomas Aquinas can well serve as a principle for developing a secular liturgy. Before attempting this, let me show how the history of religions reveals a view of worship which is the very opposite of this principle.

"Worship" has come to be used interchangeably wtih "liturgy." The latter term comes from the Greek, *leitourgia,* which first signified any kind of public duty, not only the religious kind. It later came to mean the public service rendered to God in a temple. Worship, then, meant, in contrast with the above principle, *placating* a basically hostile God with offerings, ceremonies and sacrifices. Attendance at a liturgical function was the fulfillment of an obligation to God. God changed from being hostile to friendly when he was given the worship due him. While all

of this is understandable and acceptable
when taken metaphorically, it has often been
taken literally even by many people today.

That God was placated by man's worship
was the general understanding in ancient
times. Even the newly-formed Hebrew nation, influenced as it was by its neighboring
nations, regarded the worship of God in this
way. But it was not long before the prophets
of Yahweh began telling the people that
their worship of God was merely external
and superstitious; that God does not take
delight in burnt-offerings, but in obedience
to his voice; that worship essentially involves
being good and doing good to others (see
1 Sam. 15:22-23, Ps. 40:7-9, 49:13). The
prophets did not mean that ethical behavior
is identical with worship, but that worship is
meaningless without an essential reference
to it.

Before leaving this discussion of superstitious worship, it is necessary to make some
observations about worship in the church
today. The whole of the present ceremonial
of the mass seems to encourage the popular
theistic idea of God that I described earlier

and appears to be based on the erroneous
idea of a split between the sacred and the secular. There is the sanctuary, a "sacred place"
which gives access to the "sacred space" in
which God dwells. (Moving the altar to the
center of the church changes that symbolism
somewhat.) The priest wears sacred vestments which set him apart from the people
who wear ordinary clothes. The prayers and
other liturgical texts emphasize the other
world, the next life, and encourage indi-
vidualistic piety ("*my* meditation on the
divine mysteries"; "*my* union with Jesus
when I receive communion"). The church
building itself is a sacred place where one
withdraws from the world in order to worship God. Every other place and space outside that building is considered distinctly
secular and profane.

Given such physical and ceremonial structures, and also taking into account the pietistic, juridical and legalistic tone of pre-
Vatican II religious instruction, it is easy to
see how the people have come to think in
terms of their "obligation" of going to mass
on Sundays and holy days and understand

how they have come to believe that they
are literally "pleasing God," changing his
state from one of displeasure to one of
pleasure by fulfilling the obligation, and that
they incur the threat of punishment when
they do not fulfill the obligation. Many confess missing mass, even when they were
legitimately impeded, just to be on the safe
side. Attending mass, for many people, satis-
fies a fixated childhood desire for magical
experiences. Challenging homilies notwith-
standing, many people see only vaguely, if
at all, the essential connection there should
be between ethical conduct and worship.

In working toward a description of a secular liturgy, the working basis must be the
secular theology of God, Christ and the
church; for we worship God in Christ as
church. The only experience we can have of
God is indirect, that is, through secular
realities which contain within themselves a
God-given sacred dimension. We experience
God as going before us when we are on the
boundary between the secular and its sacred
dimension. We place ourselves on that boundary by responding in faith to God's call in

the redeemer, Christ, who himself *is* that boundary.

The church is the true body of Christ when its whole concern and reason for being is not its own institutional well-being and progress, but its service to the world and man so that they can develop, becoming fully themselves in their progress toward the God of our future.

What would be the shape and style of a liturgy growing out of such a secular theology? There is no longer any question of the *need* for revision and renewal of the liturgy. Vatican II has acknowledged secularization as a fact, and has shown that the church is ready to live and work in a creative way (see *Pastoral Constitution on the Church in the Modern World*, nn. 21, 36, 39, 40, 41). The same council desired that "the rites be carefully and thoroughly revised in the light of sound tradition, and that they be given new vigor to meet the circumstances and needs of modern times" (*Constitution on the Sacred Liturgy*, n. 4; see also nn. 21, 34, 37, 40). The mandate is clear and the challenge is impelling.

A secular liturgy should not take place in a church building. Christians of the first three centuries had no churches or altars. Such an edifice is considered to be a sacred place, apart from the world. It militates against the need for finding and liberating the sacred dimension of any building, which is basically secular. Any other place but a church should be the locus for cultus if the place is ordinarily considered a worldly place. This could be in a home or in a school or in a public building or anywhere else where other meetings are held for non-sacred purposes.

Secondly, the priest should not wear vestments that set him apart from the people. Nor should the furniture and vessels and other objects be specially consecrated and set aside *only* for liturgical use. They should be things used in the course of everyday living, so that their sacred dimension can be discovered and affirmed by the worshiping community.

Thirdly, the form of the activity of secular worship should be basically and more obviously that of a meal. The simple and deciding reason for this is that Jesus did it that way. Jesus did not celebrate the last supper in a temple or synagogue, nor did he wear special vestments or use consecrated vessels.

Why did Jesus choose the form of a meal? This particular human act among families and friends is most suited for signifying the love-unity of those eating together. It also provides the sustenance, spiritual as well as material, for conserving and deepening that unity. The spiritual sustenance of this love-unity is the attitude of thankfulness to God for the unspeakable gift of being able to love unselfishly, thereby effecting this unity. It also creates the experience of joy and peace which accompany such a unity.

Vatican II teaches that Jesus is present during the eucharistic meal in the scripture that is read, in the consecrated bread and wine, and by reason of the fact that the people are gathered together *in his name* (see *ibid*, n. 7). We are also reminded by the same council that, in the eucharistic celebration, we "proclaim the death of the Lord until he comes" (1 Cor. 11:26). Why the *death* of the Lord? Because by his death Jesus destroyed all hostility in his very person (see Eph. 2:14-16), thereby showing us the way of dying to ourselves in order to live for others, thus promoting love-unity in the world. If Jesus is present in the announcement of the scripture and in the consecrated bread and wine, he is not necessarily present in the people *come together in his name,* unless the individuals present have achieved some measure of love-unity, however imperfectly, among themselves. Otherwise, the ultimate signification and effect of Jesus' presence in the consecrated bread and wine, namely, the love-unity of the body of worshipers, is frustrated. "If, when you are bringing your gift to the altar, you suddenly remember that your brother has a grievance against you, leave your gift where it is before the altar. First go and make your peace with your brother, and only then come back and offer your gift" (Mt. 5:23-24). The minimum for the real presence of Jesus in the people gathered together in his name is that each individual be involved in secular concerns following the way of the secular Christ: in serving the poor, the hungry, the thirsty, the sick and those who are in prison, and in breaking down the hostilities between men and communities and even nations by self-sacrificing love and service.

A secular liturgy has an ethical content. If there has been no doing good for others, no contribution to the building up of the world, not even any compunction for the neglect to be so engaged or any desire to amend, *there is no cause for celebration.* We cannot render *leitourgia* or public service to God directly, but only through rendering service to the secular—liberating in it that sacred dimension which points to God going before the pilgrim-world.

A secular liturgy, then, should take place in a secular place, in secular dress, with secular things and, whenever possible, with a generous use of contemporary secular forms of music, dance, film and drama. This perhaps is the place for making some suggestions which may be even more concrete.

The eucharistic liturgy can well be preceded by a brief communal penance service, that is, a rite of reconciliation, because every member of the worshiping community will have come with some failing which has caused "a brother to have a grievance against him." Quite aside from personal failure, there is the "sin of the world" for which the whole community ought to feel some guilt and consequently compunction and purpose of amendment and the need for reconciliation. The service can consist of brief scripture readings which reveal the reality of private and corporate sin; a general confession made by the priest of selected private and corporate sins of which the group would most likely accuse itself, and a confession of certain sins by any individual who might spontaneously feel the rightness of doing so.

Then, after a communal expression of contrition, a public sacramental absolution takes place. The value of such communal confession over private confession is that it more clearly signifies the reconciliation ("first go and make peace with your brother") that should exist in the community *before* that community celebrates the eucharist, which should signify a reconciliation already achieved. This concelebrated penance could become the accepted practice, without, however, eliminating the availability of private

confession for any penitent who had a personal problem or a need for special counseling
by a priest.

The worshiping community should be
small enough so that the people comprising
it know each other on a first-name basis. The
group can be heterogeneous in regard to age,
sex, occupation and apostolate. The advantage in this kind of grouping would be the
sharing of a variety of christian services to
the world. The group can also be homogene-
ous. It could be made up of real-estate
brokers working together for fair-housing
practices, or of lawyers or physicians who
render service to the poor and illiterate, or
of factory workers and semi-skilled laborers
who work for better conditions for their
fellow workers.

What is important about having a small
and personal worshiping group is that the
liturgy of the Word also includes a word
about what the people, both as individuals
and as a group, have been doing "to make
the Word become flesh in their society," and
what they must yet do to bring the incarnation to fuller realization. This could well

take place in the dialogue-homily where many of those present could contribute in- terpretations, suggestions and insights on a scriptural passage, relating it to their daily life of christian service to the world and man. People, then, would not come to the liturgy empty-handed but willing to face their worldly duties as christians.

The offertory procession would have more meaning and relevance, because the bread and wine offered would represent the *real* sacrifices of those present who have been working in definite apostolates to further the gospel's message in the world. The prayer over the gifts would be a petition that the people's sacrifices, at first represented by the bread and wine, be changed into Christ's own self-sacrifice by means of the consecra- tion of the bread and wine.

The ethical actions of the people in favor of the secular would become acts of worship. It is through Jesus, the mediator, that we have access to the Father in order to thank and praise him for being able to make a gift of ourselves, and to ask him for his con- tinuous grace to do so.

Then would we have the real *communion* of the faithful together in Christ, a new event previously signified by Christ's becoming present under the appearances of the bread and wine. There would be a communion and at the same time a sign to the rest of the world of what it could become if it were to become christian.

In addition, individuals should take the consecrated bread and cup into their own hands and communicate themselves, rather than receive them from the hands of the priest. The latter practice suggests a father/ child relationship, which is out of place in a worshiping community of adult christians.

I have said that the worshiping community is a sign to the world. The nonbeliever may not perceive anything sacred about the church's work of service in the world, but it *can* become visible to him in the church's liturgical *celebration* of that service. It is during such a time that the church can show how the "secular-secular" of the nonbeliever has a sacred dimension which causes it to be more "sacred-secular." This, in turn, becomes the content of a celebration which is "sacred-sacred" (see the table in Chapter Two, p. 37).

The secular liturgy should often make use of contemporary media, focusing attention on secular realities which are the necessary object of ethical concern and of christian worship. Music, dance, film and drama would not only be highly instructional, but would also dispel the solemnity which has too long characterized liturgical worship, presupposing a distant, hostile, unapproachable God who needs our reverence and worship. We have for too long accepted the principles that it is unimportant if the liturgy doesn't "do" anything to you. In fact, it is more meritorious to celebrate it when it doesn't. This is wholly false, contradicting what we have already accepted as true, namely, that God does not need our worship, but *we* need to worship God. How can the church, which has read the 150th Psalm over and over again, remain completely unaffected by it in her liturgical expression?

O Praise ye the Lord!
Praise God in his sanctuary . . .

Praise him with the sound of the trumpet!
Praise him with the lute and the harp!
Praise him with timbrels and dance!
Praise him upon the strings and pipes!
Praise him upon the loud cymbals!
Praise him upon the high-sounding
    cymbals!

What if our liturgy did accept the seemingly irreverent invitation of the 47th Psalm: "Clap your *hands*, all peoples! Shout to God with loud shouts of joy!"? The liturgy should be happy, light-hearted and even playful, because the death of the Lord we proclaim is a death which has swallowed up death and has given us the hope that developing the goodness-potential of *this* world and *this* life is the very way to the future kingdom of God.

A secular liturgy, therefore, will give praise to the loving and saving power of the secular God, using every achievement of art and science and technology, every exploration into outer space, every struggle against poverty, oppression, racism and economic inequality among nations, every single struggle which results in lifting people up to a higher level of human living.

A secular liturgy will also signify the readiness, zeal and restlessness of the people of God to continue to serve the world until every secret of nature is unlocked, until every potential of earth and outer space is realized, until the whole secular world becomes united in love in a kingdom of freedom, peace and joy. For "then comes the end when [Jesus] delivers up the kingdom to God the Father, after abolishing every kind of domination, authority and power . . . and when all things are subject to him, then the Son himself will also be made subordinate to God who made all things subject to him, and thus God will be all in all" (1 Cor. 15:24-28).

SOURCES

Ahern, Barnabas. *The Formation of the Scripture*. Chicago: Argus Communications, 1967, pp. 37, 62.

DuBay, William. *The Human Church*. Garden City, N.Y.: Doubleday, 1966, pp. 108-110, 112, 128.

DISCUSSION QUESTIONS

1. Would we lose the sense of the sacred if we celebrated mass without vestments, incense, and other "sacred" props?

2. What is the paschal mystery? Is the sacrament of penance a part of that paschal mystery? What are the implications for the liturgy?

3. How often should mass be celebrated?

4. If mass were to be celebrated in many small groups, how solve the problem of the shortage of priests?

5. Every liturgical celebration should have ethical content. What does this mean?

6. Do you think someone should participate in a mass if he is working against racial justice?

Suggested Readings

Duquoc, Christian, Editor. *Spirituality in the Secular City.* (*Concilium,* Vol. XIX) Glen Rock, N.J.: Paulist Press, 1966.

Loen, Arnold. *Secularization.* London: SCM Press, 1967.

Mascall, Eric. *The Secularization of Christianity.* New York: Holt, Rinehart and Winston, 1966.

Meland, Bernard. *The Secularization of Modern Cultures.* New York: Oxford University Press, 1966.

Metz, Johannes, ed. *The Church and the World.* (*Concilium,* Vol. VI) Glen Rock, N.J.: Paulist Press, 1965.

Rahner, Karl, and Schillebeeckx, Edward, Editors. *The Church and Mankind.* (*Concilium,* Vol. I) Glen Rock, N.J.: Paulist Press, 1965.

Ramsey, A. M. *Sacred and Secular.* New York: Harper and Row, 1965.

Richard, Robert. *Secularization Theology.* New York: Herder and Herder, 1967.

Richardson, Alan. *History Sacred and Profane.* Philadelphia: Westminster Press, 1964.

Smith, Ronald G. *Secular Christianity.* New York: Harper and Row, 1966.

Wicker, Brian. *Toward a Contemporary Christianity.* Notre Dame, Indiana: University of Notre Dame Press, 1967.

Williams, Colin. *Faith in a Secular Age.* New York: Harper and Row, 1966.

Multi-Media

The Church in the World. Loneliness, fear, lack of concern and social evils are the challenge for the church today. The film brings christianity to every aspect of human life. *Augsburg Publishing House, 426 S. Fifth Street, Minneapolis, Minnesota 55415. 24 minutes. Black and White. Rent $20.*

Men for Others. This film shows members of the Woodlawn Organization in Chicago and Peace Corp workers in Africa. The camera observes people interested in the welfare of their fellow men and the various ways these individuals are serving others through spiritual, social and economic channels. *NET Film Service, Indiana University, Audio-Visual Center, Bloomington, Indiana 47401. 60 minutes. Black and White. Rent $9.15.*

The Men in Black. This is a study of the relationships between the clergy and the catholic people of Ireland. The film includes an examination of criticisms that the church is too authoritative and conservative and out of touch with the people it serves. *NET Film Service, Indiana University, Audio-Visual Cen-*

ter, *Bloomington, Indiana 47401. 60 minutes. Black and White. Rent $9.15.*

Of Stars and Men. This film drives home to the viewer that he cannot consider himself the center of the universe as his ancestors did. Knowledge has proven to man that he cannot live by superstitions; now he must stand up to the universe as man. *Brandon Films, Inc., 221 West 57th Street, New York, N. Y. 10019. 53 minutes. Color. Rent $35.*

Of Time, Work and Leisure. The film argues forcefully that work may make man rich and even noble; leisure perfects him. Leisure is freedom, freedom from the domination of time, freedom from the necessity of work. The film presents what should humanize man and quiet his spirit. *NET Film Service, Indiana University, Audio-Visual Center, Bloomington, Indiana 47401. 30 minutes. Black and White. Rent. $5.40.*

Parable. The story is an allegorical portrayal of Christ. The entire film is a parable epitomizing the history of mankind and of each individual. The lifetime task of each man is to find meaning in and the purpose of his life. Although the symbols are almost dense, the film portrays the metamorphosis of a christian. It is a modern commentary on the person of Christ and every man. *Contemporary Films, Inc., 828 Custer Avenue, Evanston, Illinois 60202. 22 minutes. Color. Rent $20.*

Religious Revolution and the Void. This film examines the revolution that exists within some parts of the church which sees the church involving itself in such matters as civil rights, jazz, dancing, and the new forms of social work, in an effort to identify with young people and hopefully bring them back to organized religion. *NET Film Service, Indiana University, Audio-Visual Center, Bloomington, Indiana 47401. 60 minutes. Black and White. Rent $9.15.*

The Revolution in Human Expectations. Describing the needs of underdeveloped areas of the world and how they often produce violence, this film analyzes demands by people in so-called backward areas and investigates what should be done both now and in the future to foster development of these areas. *NET Film Service, Indiana University, Audio-Visual Center, Bloomington, Indiana 47401. 30 minutes. Black and White. Rent $5.40.*

Universe. This exciting visual exploration of the vast universe is a projection into the realms of time and space which stuns the imagination. The film stimulates a real sensitivity to and appreciation of God as Creator. *Contemporary Films, Inc., 828 Custer Avenue, Evanston, Illinois 60202. 28 Minutes. Black and White. Rent $8.*

The Young Americans. A study of youth in America—who they are, what they want, where they fit in, how they affect society, what they believe in and why. *NET Film Service, Indiana University, Bloomington, Indiana 47401. 30 minutes. Black and White. Rent $5.40.*

The Death of God. Whose God is dead? Does God change? How can man have a personal relationship with a god who does not change?

Part I Norris Clarke, S.J., and Avery Dulles, S.J.
Price: 33/4 I.P.S.—$5.75. 17/8 I.P.S.—$4.30.

Part II: James Shenkel, S.J., and Avery Dulles, S.J.
Price: 33/4 I.P.S.—$5.75. 17/8 I.P.S.—$4.30. Argus Communications, 3505 North Ashland Avenue, Chicago, Illinois 60657.

God, Revolution and the City. Dr. Marty speaks on the Child of Promise, the City of the Future, the God who promises and the Politics of the Church and the Revolution of the World. *Price: 33/4 I.P.S.—$5.75. 17/8 I.P.S.—$4.30. Argus Communications, 3505 North Ashland Avenue, Chicago, Illinois 60657.*